ACKNOWLEDGEMENTS

To Dr. Robert Andrews, University of Colorado Ornithologist

Birds of Prey Rehabilitation Foundation

Richard Holmes, Marie and Paul West

and

Family members Paul Echternacht, Ralph Seacrest and Violet McNew for, above all, patience— and for computer instruction and use.

Second Edition

1990 and 1993 by Betty R. Seacrest

& Delbert A. McNew

Produced by Avery Press, Inc.
600 Kalmia Ave.,
Boulder, CO 80304

Designed by Molly Gough
3675 Buckeye Ct.,
Boulder, CO 80304

Distributed by Johnson Books
1880 S. 57th Ct.,
Boulder, CO 80301

Front cover: Clark's Nutcracker (*Nucifraga Columbiana*) and Steller's Jay (*Cyanocitta Stelleri*)

Library of Congress Catalog Card Number: 90-83462

Printed in Hong Kong

ISBN 0-937321-01-X

TABLE OF CONTENTS
(Index of Common Names, p. 100)
Predominant Color(s) of Male

	Pages		Pages
Black.	1-7	**Gray.**	65-78
and Orange	8	and Brown.	79
and White.	9-17	and Red.	80
and Yellow.	18-19	and White.	81-84
Blue.	20-22	and Yellow.	85-86
and Buff.	23	**White.**	87-88
and Rust.	24-25	**Yellow.**	89
and White.	26-28	and Black.	90-92
-Gray and Rust.	29	**Miscellaneous**	
-Gray and White.	30-31	Copper.	93
Brown.	32-46	Green.	94
and Gray.	47-48	Red and Brown.	95-97
and White.	49-62	Rust.	98
and Yellow	63-64	Rust and White.	99

Sizes given are apparent sizes as seen in the field, NOT ornithologist measured-by-the-ruler sizes. Handheld birds are about to be released, having been banded under the auspices of the Colorado Bird Observatory.

Photography is by the Authors except for the following:
Hugh Kingery: p. 6a; Michael Linshaw, M.D.: p. 961; Charles W. Melton: p.241; Stephen Keith: p. 36.

EUROPEAN STARLING
Sturnus vulgaris
6 inches (15 cm.)

WINGS are black.
HEAD is iridescent black.
BILL is yellow.
NECK is iridescent black.
BREAST is iridescent black.
BACK is black; tail is short.
SEXES are alike.
FEEDS by gleaning.
EATS insects, berries and seeds.
NESTS in any cavity it can find.
FLOCKS with other birds, mostly
blackbirds.
WINTERS in the region.
PLUMAGE CAN VARY GREATLY
WITH AGE AND SEASON.

BLACK

BLACK/Evergreens

WILLIAMSON'S SAPSUCKER
Sphyrapicus thyroideus
8-1/4 inches (21 cm.)

WINGS have a white patch.
HEAD has narrow white stripes.
BILL is long and black.
NECK has a red throat patch.
BREAST is black; belly is yellow.
BACK is black with a white rump,
black tail.
FEMALE is brown, with a barred
back, black bib.
FEEDS by probing tree bark.
EATS insects and seeds.
NESTS in a tree cavity.
WINTERS south of Colorado.
BOTH SEXES HAVE A YELLOW
BELLY.

BREWER'S BLACKBIRD
Euphagus cyanocephalus
9 inches (23 cm.)

WINGS are glossy black with a green tint.
HEAD is glossy black with a purple tint.
NECK is black with a purple tint.
BREAST is black with a green tint.
BACK is glossy black with a green tint.
EYES are yellow.
FEMALE is browner, has brown eyes.
FEEDS by gleaning foliage and ground.
EATS insects and seeds.
NESTS in trees or shrubs.
WINTERS usually south of Colorado.
MIGRATES into Montana by late April.
WILL FORM HUGE FLOCKS WITH OTHER TYPES OF BLACKBIRDS.

3

BLACK/Varied: deserts to mountains

COMMON RAVEN
Corvus corax
21 inches (53 cm.)

WINGS are black.
HEAD is black.
BILL is heavy, Roman-nosed.
NECK is black, with shaggy
feathers.
BREAST is black.
BACK is black; tail is wedge-
shaped.
SEXES are alike.
FEEDS on the ground.
EATS, primarily, carrion.
NESTS in trees or on cliffs.
FLOCKS in the winter.
WINTERS in the region.
THE RAVEN IS ONE OF OUR
MOST INTELLIGENT AND
ADAPTABLE BIRDS.

RED-WINGED BLACKBIRD
Agelaius phoeniceus
8-3/4 inches (22 cm.)

WINGS are black with a red-and-buff shoulder.
HEAD is black.
NECK is black.
BREAST is black.
BACK is black; tail is black.
FEMALE is brown with a streaked breast.
FEEDS in foliage and gleans.
EATS insects and seeds.
NESTS in reeds or cattails.
WINTERS from Colorado south.
MIGRATES into Montana by February.
POSSIBLY THE MOST NUMEROUS NORTH AMERICAN LAND BIRD.

5

BLACK

BLACK/Woodlands, farmlands, urban areas

BROWN-HEADED COWBIRD
Molothrus ater
7-1/2 inches (19 cm.)

WINGS are black.
HEAD is brown.
NECK is brown.
BREAST is metallic green-black.
BACK is metallic green-black.
FEMALE is grayish-brown.
FEEDS on the ground.
EATS insects and seeds.
WINTERS in the southern border
states and Mexico.
MIGRATES into Montana by late April.
THE BROWN-HEADED COWBIRD IS
A SOCIAL PARASITE, LAYING ITS
EGGS IN THE NESTS OF OTHER
BIRDS.

AMERICAN CROW
Corvus brachyrhynchos
17 inches (23 cm.)

WINGS are black.
HEAD is black.
NECK is smooth and black.
BREAST is black.
BACK is black; tail is black.
SEXES are alike.
FEEDS on the ground.
EATS anything. Omnivorous.
NESTS in trees and shrubs.
WINTERS in the southern Rockies.
MIGRATES into Montana by mid-March.
CROWS CAW; RAVENS CROAK.
RAVENS SOAR; CROWS DO NOT.
RAVENS HAVE SHAGGY FOREHEAD
AND THROAT; CROWS DO NOT.

BLACK & ORANGE/Woodlands

BLACK-HEADED GROSBEAK
Pheucticus melanocephalus
7-1/4 inches (18 cm.)

WINGS are black with white bars.
HEAD is black
BILL is heavy; color inconspicuous.
NECK is black.
BREAST, lower throat orange.
BACK streaked; rump orange.
FEMALE has a brown striped head,
buff breast.
FEEDS by gleaning foliage and
ground.
EATS insects, seeds, and fruit.
NESTS in shrubs.
WINTERS in Mexico.
MIGRATES into Montana by mid-May.
SOMETIMES SINGS WHILE INCU-
BATING. GROSBEAK MEANS "FAT
BEAK".

DOWNY (HAIRY? See below) WOODPECKER
Picoides pubescens
5 inches (12 cm.)

WINGS are black and white.
HEAD is black and white with a red patch.
BILL is long and thin.
NECK is white.
BREAST is white.
BACK is white.
FEMALE lacks red nape patch.
FEEDS by gleaning and excavating tree bark.
EATS insects.
NESTS in a tree cavity.
WINTERS in the Rockies.
HAIRY WOODPECKER IS ALMOST IDENTICAL IN APPEARANCE TO, BUT 1/3 LARGER THAN, THE DOWNY.

9

BLACK

BLACK & WHITE/Lakes, rivers

COMMON MERGANSER
Mergus merganser
18 inches (46 cm.)

WINGS are white.
HEAD is dark green.
BILL is red.
NECK is dark green.
BREAST and belly are white.
LEGS are red.
BACK is black.
FEMALE has a rust, crested head, gray back.
FEEDS by diving.
EATS fish.
NESTS in a cavity or crevice.
WINTERS in the region.
ONE OF THE MOST COMMON DUCKS IN THE MOUNTAINS.

RUFOUS-SIDED TOWHEE
Pipilo erythrophthalmus.
7-1/4 inches (18 cm.)

WINGS are black with white bars and spots.
HEAD is black.
NECK is black.
BREAST is white with rufous sides.
EYES are red.
FEMALE is brown where male is black.
FEEDS by gleaning foliage and ground, mostly.
EATS insects, seeds, and berries.
NESTS in shrubs.
FLOCKS in the winter.
WINTERS, sometimes, in region; mostly migratory.
MIGRATES into Montana by late May.
OFTEN BATHES IN THE DEW OR FOG DROPS ON VEGETATION.

11

BLACK

BLACK & WHITE/Wetlands

AMERICAN AVOCET

Recurvirostra americana
15 inches (38 cm.)

WINGS are black with a white stripe.
HEAD is pinkish tan.
BILL very long, black, upcurved.
NECK is long and pinkish tan.
BREAST is pinkish-tan, belly is white.
LEGS are long and blue.
BACK is black and white.
EYES have a white ring.
SEXES are alike.
FEEDS by sweeping bill under water.
EATS aquatic insects, plants, seeds.
NESTS on the ground .
WINTERS on coasts of Calif., Mexico.
MIGRATES into Montana by mid-
April.
WILSON'S PHALAROPES FOLLOW
AVOCETS, FEED ON THE INSECTS
STIRRED UP.

COMMON GOLDENEYE
Bucephala clangula
13 inches (33 cm.)

WINGS are dark gray with white patches.
HEAD is green with a white spot below the eye.
NECK is white.
BREAST is white.
BACK is black.
EYES are golden.
FEMALE is grayish with a dark-brown head, white neck.
FEEDS by diving.
EATS aquatic insects, crayfish and fish.
NESTS in a tree cavity near water.
THE GOLDENEYE IS A YEAR-AROUND RESIDENT IN THE ROCKY MOUNTAIN STATES.

13

BLACK

BLACK & WHITE/Wetlands

WESTERN GREBE
Aechmorphus occidentalis
18 inches (46 cm.)

WINGS are black.
HEAD has a black crown and white cheeks.
BILL is yellow.
NECK is long and swan-like.
BREAST is white.
BACK is black.
EYES are red.
SEXES are alike.
FEEDS by diving.
EATS fish.
NESTS on water in vegetation.
FLOCKS in large colonies.
WINTERS along the Pacific coast.
MIGRATES into Montana in May.
THE COURTSHIP DANCES ARE SPECTACULAR; OFTEN THE WHOLE FLOCK PARTICIPATES.

BLACK-BILLED MAGPIE
Pica pica
16 inches (41 cm.)

WINGS are greenish-black and white.
HEAD is black.
NECK is black.
BREAST is black; belly is white.
BACK is black; tail is very long,
iridescent black.
SEXES are alike.
FEEDS by gleaning.
EATS insects and carrion.
NESTS in trees.
FLOCKS in the winter.
WINTERS in the region.
HAS A CALIFORNIA COUSIN CALLED
THE "YELLOW-BILLED MAGPIE".

15

BLACK

BLACK & WHITE/Woodlands

RED-NAPED SAPSUCKER
Sphyrapicus nuchalis
8 inches (20 cm.)

WINGS are black with a white patch.
HEAD is striped black-and-white with
red patches.
BILL is long and narrow.
NECK has a red throat patch.
BREAST light yellow with black bib.
BACK black-and-white striped; tail
black with white rump
FEMALE has white chin.
FEEDS by excavating small holes in
trees.
EATS insects and sap.
NESTS in a tree cavity.
WINTERS usually south of Colorado.
MIGRATES into Montana by mid-
April.
OLD NEST CAVITIES ARE USED BY
MANY OTHER SPECIES.

BLACK-CAPPED CHICKADEE
Parus atricapillus
4-1/2 inches (11 cm.)

WINGS are gray.
HEAD has a black cap and white cheeks.
NECK has a black throat patch.
BREAST is white.
BACK is gray.
SEXES are alike.
FEEDS by gleaning.
EATS Insects and seeds.
NESTS in a tree cavity, nestboxes.
FLOCKS in the winter.
WINTERS in the region.
RARELY NESTS IN CONIFER TREES.

17

BLACK

BLACK & YELLOW/Mixed woods

EVENING GROSBEAK
Coccothraustes vespertinus
7-1/4 inches (18 cm.)

WINGS have a white patch.
HEAD has a yellow forehead and eyebrow.
BILL is short, massive, and light-colored.
NECK is olive-brown.
BREAST is dull yellow.
BACK is dull yellow.
FEMALE plumage is dull grayish-tan.
FEEDS by gleaning.
EATS seeds, fruit, tree sap.
NESTS high in trees.
FLOCKS after the breeding season.
WINTERS in the region.
MIGRATES within the region.
VERY TAME. FREQUENT FEEDER VISITOR.

YELLOW-HEADED BLACKBIRD
Xanthocephalus xanthocephalus
9-1/2 inches (24 cm.)

WINGS are black with a white patch.
HEAD is yellow.
NECK is yellow.
BREAST is yellow; belly is black.
BACK is black.
FEMALE is brown with yellow throat
and breast.
FEEDS in foliage and gleans.
EATS insects, and seeds.
NESTS in reeds and cattails.
WINTERS in Mexico.
MIGRATES into Montana by late April.
THE ONLY NORTH AMERICAN BIRD
WITH A YELLOW HEAD AND BLACK
BODY.

19

BLACK

BLUE/Evergreens

STELLER'S JAY
Cyanocitta stelleri
11 inches (28 cm.)

WINGS are blue with a black shoulder.
HEAD is black.
NECK is black.
BREAST is brown to blue.
BACK is dark gray with a blue rump
and tail.
EYES have white eyebrows.
SEXES are alike.
FEEDS by gleaning.
EATS seeds, insects, bird eggs.
NESTS in trees.
WINTERS in the region.
HYBRIDIZES WITH BLUE JAY ALONG
FRONT RANGE IN COLO. HAUNTS
PICNIC AREAS, CAMPSITES.

BLUE/Evergreens, meadows, open rangelands over 5,000'

MOUNTAIN BLUEBIRD
Sialia currucoides
7-1/4 inches (18 cm.)

WINGS are blue.
HEAD is blue.
NECK is blue.
BREAST is pale blue.
BACK is blue.
FEMALE is gray-brown on back and breast.
FEEDS by hovering and pouncing, gleaning.
EATS insects, also some fruit.
NESTS in tree cavities, nestboxes, fences.
WINTERS in southwestern U.S. and Mexico.
MIGRATES into Montana by mid-March.
TWO BROODS A SEASON OVER MUCH OF THEIR RANGE.

21

BLUE

BLUE

BLUE/Woodlands, scrub oak, chaparral

SCRUB JAY
Aphelocoma coerulescens
11 inches (28 cm.)

WINGS are blue.
HEAD is blue, black eye patch.
NECK is blue with whitish throat.
BREAST is white.
BACK is brown.
SEXES are alike.
FEEDS by gleaning.
EATS acorns, insects, eggs, nestlings.
NESTS in shrubs.
WINTERS in the region.
RARE IN MONTANA, WYOMING AND
IDAHO.

BLUE & BUFF/Around humans, especially bridges and culverts.

BARN SWALLOW
Hirundo rustica
6 inches (15 cm.)

WINGS are blue-black.
HEAD is blue-black.
NECK is blue-black.
BREAST is buff.
BACK is blue-black with a deeply forked tail.
FEMALE plumage is duller.
FEEDS by catching insects in flight.
EATS insects.
NESTS on buildings and bridges.
FLOCKS in small colonies.
WINTERS in Central and South America.
MIGRATES into Montana by late April.
ADULTS RETURN TO THE SAME NEST EVERY YEAR.

23

BLUE

BLUE & RUST/Open woodlands, farmlands, orchards

WESTERN BLUEBIRD
Sialia mexicana
7 inches (18 cm.)

WINGS are blue.
HEAD is blue.
NECK is blue.
BREAST is chestnut.
BACK is chestnut.
FEMALE plumage is duller.
FEEDS by hunting from a perch. Also gleans.
EATS Insects, worms, and berries.
NESTS often in woodpecker-excavated hole, posts, nestboxes.
WINTERS in the desert Southwest and Mexico.
MIGRATES into Montana by mid-March.
SONG NOT AS MELODIOUS AS THAT OF THE EASTERN BLUEBIRD.

BLUE & RUST/Woodlands, bushy areas near water

LAZULI BUNTING
Passerina amoena
5-1/2 inches (14 cm.)

WINGS are black and white.
HEAD is blue.
BILL is short and heavy.
NECK is blue.
BREAST and sides are cinnamon; belly
is white.
BACK is blue.
FEMALE is brown.
FEEDS in foliage and gleans.
EATS insects and seeds.
NESTS in brush.
WINTERS in Mexico.
MIGRATES into Montana by mid-May.
SONG SIMILAR TO THAT OF INDIGO
BUNTING OF EASTERN U.S.

25

BLUE

BLUE AND WHITE/Evergreens

VIOLET-GREEN SWALLOW

Tachycineta thalassina
5 inches (13 cm.)

WINGS are green-black.
HEAD is green-black. White cheeks extend above eyes.
NECK is green-black.
BREAST is white.
BACK is green-black with white sides to rump.
FEMALE is duller.
FEEDS by catching flying insects.
EATS insects.
NESTS in a tree cavity or rock crevice.
FLOCKS occasionally with tree swallows.
WINTERS mainly in Mexico.
MIGRATES into Montana in April.
USUALLY NESTS IN ABANDONED WOODPECKER HOLES.

GREAT BLUE HERON
Ardea herodias
38 inches (97 cm.)

WINGS are blue-gray.
HEAD has a black crown and plume.
BILL is long and yellow.
NECK is very long and blue-gray.
BREAST has a plume bib.
LEGS are very long.
BACK is blue-gray.
EYES are yellow.
SEXES are alike.
FEEDS by wading.
EATS fish, frogs, small mammals, food scraps.
NESTS in large cottonwoods.
FLOCKS in breeding areas.
WINTERS from southern U.S. south.
MIGRATES into Montana late March.
IN FLIGHT, CURLS ITS NECK INTO A TIGHT S.

27

BLUE

BLUE & WHITE/Woodlands

TREE SWALLOW
Tachycineta bicolor
5 inches (13 cm.)

WINGS are blue-black.
HEAD is blue-black with white cheeks.
NECK is blue-black with a white throat.
BREAST is white.
BACK is blue-black.
FEMALE is duller.
FEEDS by catching insects in flight and, rarely, gleaning.
EATS insects and berries.
NESTS in a tree cavity.
FLOCKS in the fall and spring.
WINTERS in the southern U.S. and Mexico.
MIGRATES into Mont. by early April.
USUALLY NESTS OLD WOODPECK-ER HOLES OR UNDER EAVES.

AMERICAN KESTREL
Falco sparverius
8-1/2 inches (22 cm.)

WINGS are blue-gray.
HEAD has two mustache marks on each side.
BILL is hooked.
NECK is brown.
BREAST is buffy.
BACK is rusty-brown with bars; tail is rusty with black band.
FEMALE streaked breast, dull plumage.
FEEDS by hovering and swooping.
EATS insects and small mammals.
NESTS tree cavity, often cottonwood.
WINTERS in southern U.S. and Central America.
MIGRATES into Montana in March.
ALSO CALLED SPARROW HAWK.
OFTEN PERCH ON POWER LINES.

29

BLUE

BLUE-GRAY & WHITE/Evergreens

RED-BREASTED NUTHATCH
Sitta canadensis
4 inches (10 cm.)

WINGS are gray.
HEAD is black with a white stripe above the eye.
NECK is rusty.
BREAST is rusty.
BACK is gray.
EYES have a black stripe across them.
FEMALE plumage is duller.
FEEDS by gleaning on trees.
EATS insects and seeds.
NESTS in a tree cavity.
WINTERS in the region if food is adequate.
MIGRATES but not every year.
AFTER NEST HOLE IS MADE, THE ADULTS SPREAD RESIN ABOVE AND BELOW THE HOLE.

BELTED KINGFISHER
Ceryle alcyon
12 inches (30 cm.)

WINGS are blue-gray with a black tip.
HEAD is blue-gray with a large crest.
BILL is very large.
NECK is white.
BREAST is white with a gray band.
BACK is blue-gray.
EYES have a small white spot in front.
FEMALE has a rufous breast band.
FEEDS by diving.
EATS fish and amphibians.
NESTS in a burrow near water.
WINTERS in Colorado and on south.
MIGRATES into Montana by late March.
ADULTS TEACH YOUNG TO FISH BY CRIPPLING A FISH AND DROPPING IT INTO THE WATER FOR THE YOUNG TO CATCH.

31

BLUE

BROWN/Around humans

HOUSE SPARROW
Passer domesticus
5-1/4 inches (13 cm.)

WINGS are brown.
HEAD has white cheeks, chestnut nape.
NECK has a black throat.
BREAST is gray with a black bib.
BACK is brown-streaked.
FEMALE is brown with unstreaked breast, no bib.
FEEDS by gleaning.
EATS seeds and insects.
NESTS in a cavity.
FLOCKS in the winter.
WINTERS in the region.
USURPS NESTING AREAS OF OTHER SPECIES.

GOLDEN EAGLE
Aquila chrysaetos
32 inches (81 cm.)

WINGS are brown.
HEAD is brown with a golden sheen.
BILL is large and dark.
NECK is brown with a golden sheen.
BREAST is brown.
LEGS are feathered to the toes.
BACK is brown.
EYES are brown.
SEXES are alike.
FEEDS by swooping down on its prey.
EATS small mammals, occasionally
snakes, birds, carrion.
NESTS on cliffs and in tall trees.
WINTERS in the southern Rockies.
OFTEN USE AROMATIC LEAVES IN
THE NEST TO DETER INSECT
PESTS. SOME GOLDEN EAGLES DO
NOT MIGRATE.

33

BROWN

BROWN/Diversified

ROCK WREN
Salpinctes obsoletus
4-3/4 inches (12 cm.)

WINGS are brown.
HEAD is brown.
NECK is brown.
BREAST is gray, narrowly streaked
with brown.
BACK is dark gray with a rusty rump.
SEXES are alike.
FEEDS by gleaning.
EATS insects.
NESTS in a crevice.
WINTERS in the Desert Southwest
and Mexico.
MIGRATES into Montana by late April.
OFTEN PAVES THE ENTRANCE TO
ITS NEST WITH PEBBLES. BOBS
HEAD, ESPECIALLY WHEN DIS-
TURBED.

HERMIT THRUSH
Catharus guttatus
6 inches (15 cm.)

WINGS are brown to rusty brown.
HEAD is brown.
NECK has a spotted throat.
BREAST is white and spotted.
BACK is brown with a rusty tail.
EYES have whitish eye ring.
SEXES are alike.
FEEDS by gleaning.
EATS insects, fruit.
NESTS in shrubs or low in trees.
WINTERS in Central America.
MIGRATES into Montana by late April.
HAS AN EXQUISITE FLUTE-LIKE
SONG.

35

BROWN

36

COMMON NIGHTHAWK
Chordeiles minor
9 inches (23 cm.)

WINGS are brown with white patches.
HEAD is brown.
BILL is very short.
NECK is brown with a white throat.
BREAST is brown-barred.
BACK is brown.
EYES are dark with a white eyebrow.
SEXES are alike.
FEEDS in the air.
EATS insects.
NESTS on ground.
WINTERS in South America.
MIGRATES into Montana by early June.
SITS LENGTHWISE ON LIMBS.
ACTIVE BOTH NIGHT AND DAY.

ROSY FINCH
Leucosticte arctoa
6-1/2 inches (16 cm.)

BROWN-CAPPED, GRAY-CROWNED,
AND BLACK ROSY FINCHES ARE
NOW CONSIDERED ONE SPECIES.
WINGS are brown, with a rosy tinge.
HEAD has a gray patch at back,
blackish forehead.
NECK is brown; Black has black neck.
BREAST is brown (black in Black);
belly is rosy.
BACK is brown (black in Black) with a
rosy rump.
FEMALE plumage is brown.
FEEDS by gleaning.
EATS seeds—insects in summer.
NESTS in a crevice among rocks.
FLOCKS in the winter.
WINTERS in the region.
MIGRATES into foothills in winter.

37

BROWN

BROWN/Shrublands

GREEN-TAILED TOWHEE
Pipilo chlorurus
6-1/4 inches (16 cm.)

WINGS are olive green.
HEAD has a rufous cap and gray cheeks.
NECK has a white throat.
BREAST is gray.
BACK is olive green.
SEXES are alike.
FEEDS by gleaning.
EATS insects, seeds, and berries.
NESTS in a low shrub or on the ground.
WINTERS in the Southwest and Mexico.
MIGRATES only as far north as central Montana.
PREFERS TO LIVE IN ARID REGIONS.

WHITE-TAILED PTARMIGAN
Lagopus leucurus
10 inches (25 cm.)

WINGS are white.
HEAD is brown, red over eye.
NECK is brown.
BREAST is brown; belly is white.
LEGS are white-feathered.
BACK is mottled-brown.
FEMALE plumage is duller.
FEEDS by grazing.
EATS vegetation and insects.
NESTS on the ground.
WINTERS in the region.
TURNS PURE WHITE FOR THE
WINTER. BURROWS IN SNOW FOR
FOOD AND WARMTH.

39

BROWN

BROWN/Wetlands

AMERICAN WIGEON
Anas americana
14 inches (36 cm.)

WINGS brown, white patch front edge.
HEAD gray with white crown and
green eye stripe.
BILL is gray-blue.
NECK is white with brown spots.
BREAST is ruddy-brown; belly white.
BACK is brown.
EYES are set in a green stripe.
FEMALE has mottled-gray head and
neck; gray wing patches.
FEEDS by diving and grazing.
EATS aquatics, grass, and insects.
NESTS on the ground.
WINTERS southern U.S. and Mexico.
MIGRATES into Montana by late April.
THE EGGS ARE ATTENDED ONLY BY
THE FEMALE. ALSO CALLED
BALDPATE.

BLUE-WINGED TEAL
Anas discors
11 inches (28 cm.)

WINGS have a pale blue patch.
HEAD is blue-gray with a white
crescent in front of eye.
NECK is blue-gray.
BREAST is brown-speckled.
BACK is dark brown.
FEMALE mottled-brown, has yel-
lowish legs, blue wing patch.
FEEDS by dabbling.
EATS aquatic seeds, greens, insects.
NESTS on the ground.
WINTERS in Central America.
MIGRATES into Montana by late April.
BELIEVED TO BE THE FASTEST
FLYING DUCK.

41

BROWN

BROWN/Wetlands

MALLARD
Anas platyrhynchos
16 inches (41 cm.)

WINGS have blue stripes with white borders.
HEAD is green.
NECK green with white band.
BREAST is reddish-brown.
BACK grayish-brown, white rump and black "duck-tail".
FEMALE mottled-brown, has orange bill with black markings.
FEEDS by dipping, gleaning.
EATS aquatic vegetation, insects, grass.
NESTS on ground near water.
MIGRATORY sometimes. Some do not migrate.
MALLARDS CHANGE MATES EVERY YEAR.

PIED-BILLED GREBE
Podilymbus podiceps
9 inches (23 cm.)

WINGS are brown.
HEAD is brown, black throat patch.
BILL is whitish with a black ring; in
winter tinged yellow.
NECK is brown; black chin and throat
(whitish in winter).
BREAST is gray-brown.
BACK brown. White patch under tail.
EYES are ringed with white.
SEXES are alike.
FEEDS by diving.
EATS insects, snails, fish, and frogs.
NESTS on the water in vegetation.
WINTERS southern U.S. and Mexico.
MIGRATES into Montana by late April.
YOUNG RIDE ON PARENTS' BACKS
EVEN UNDERWATER.

43

BROWN

BROWN/Woodlands

MOURNING DOVE
Zenaida macroura
10-1/2 inches (27 cm.)

WINGS brown with black spots.
HEAD is light with a small black mustache.
NECK is gray.
BREAST and throat are pinkish-gray.
LEGS are orange.
BACK is gray; tail is long and pointed.
SEXES are alike.
FEEDS on the ground.
EATS seeds.
NESTS on any solid support.
WINTERS from Colorado south.
MIGRATES into Montana by mid-April.
MOST ABUNDANT DOVE IN NORTH AMERICA.

NORTHERN FLICKER
Colaptes auratus
11 inches (28 cm.)

WINGS are brown with dark brown bars.
HEAD is brown with a red mustache.
BILL is long and thin.
NECK is gray with a black bib.
BREAST is white spotted with brown.
BACK is brown with dark brown spots.
FEMALE lacks the red mustache.
FEEDS often on the ground, probing for ants or grubs.
EATS ants and insects, also seeds, nuts, and grain.
NESTS in cavities, usually excavating its own.
WINTERS in Colorado and south.
MIGRATES into Montana in April.
EATS MORE ANTS THAN ANY OTHER NORTH AMERICAN BIRD.

45

BROWN/Woodlands, wild or urban

HOUSE WREN
Troglodytes aedon
4-1/2 inches (11 cm.)

WINGS and tail are barred-brown.
HEAD is brown.
NECK is grayish-brown.
BREAST is grayish-brown.
BACK is brown.
SEXES are alike.
FEEDS by gleaning on foliage.
EATS insects.
NESTS in a tree cavity.
WINTERS in southern U.S. and
Mexico.
MIGRATES into Montana by early
May.
HOUSE WRENS WILL USE A NEST
BOX.

BROWN & GRAY/Shrublands (willows) and tundra

WHITE-CROWNED SPARROW
Zonotrichia leucophrys
6 inches (15 cm.)

WINGS are brown with white bars.
HEAD is black-and-white striped.
NECK is gray.
BREAST is gray.
BACK is brown-streaked.
SEXES are alike.
FEEDS by gleaning.
EATS insects, seeds, and berries.
NESTS on the ground.
FLOCKS in the winter.
WINTERS in Colorado and south into
Mexico.
MIGRATES into Montana by late April.
THERE ARE FOUR SUBSPECIES
DISTINGUISHED BY MINOR
DIFFERENCES IN PLUMAGE.

BROWN

BROWN & GRAY/Wetlands, mountain meadows

LINCOLN'S SPARROW
Melospiza lincolnii
4-3/4 inches (12 cm.)

WINGS are brown.
HEAD is brown with gray stripes.
NECK is gray.
BREAST is buffy.
BACK is brown-striped.
EYES have a narrow ring.
SEXES are alike.
FEEDS by ground gleaning.
EATS insects and seeds.
NESTS in the grass.
WINTERS south into Central America.
MIGRATES into Montana by mid-May.
AN UNOBTRUSIVE, FURTIVE BIRD.

48

PRAIRIE FALCON
Falco mexicanus
16 inches (41 cm.)

WINGS are light brown with dark brown spots.
HEAD is light brown with a prominent mustache.
BILL is hooked.
NECK is brown.
BREAST is white with brown spots.
LEGS are feathered to the feet.
BACK light brown, dark brown spots.
FEMALE is about one-third larger than the male.
FEEDS by swooping on flying birds.
EATS birds, small mammals, and occasional insects.
NESTS on cliffs facing open habitat.
WINTERS as far north as Wyoming.
SOME PRAIRIE FALCONS DO NOT MIGRATE.

49

BROWN

BROWN & WHITE/Diversified, within range of water

BALD EAGLE
Haliaeetus leucocephalus
32 inches (81 cm.)

WINGS are brown.
HEAD is white.
BILL is yellow and very large.
NECK is white.
BREAST is brown.
LEGS are feathered almost to the feet.
BACK is brown; tail is white.
EYES are yellow.
SEXES look alike.
FEMALE is often larger than the male.
FEEDS by fishing with feet, foraging.
EATS fish, small mammals, carrion.
NESTS in tall trees or on cliffs.
WINTERS in Rockies into Canada.
ADOPTED AS OUR NATIONAL
EMBLEM IN 1782. POPULATIONS IN
ALL AREAS VARY WITH THE
SEASONS.

PINE SISKIN
Carduelis pinus
4 inches (10 cm.)

WINGS are brown with a touch of yellow.
HEAD is brown-streaked.
NECK is brown-streaked.
BREAST is brown, streaked with white.
BACK is brown-streaked.
FEMALE plumage is duller.
FEEDS by gleaning.
EATS seeds and insects.
NESTS in trees.
FLOCKS in the winter.
WINTERS in the Rockies.
OFTEN FLOCKS WITH GOLD-FINCHES.

51

BROWN

BROWN & WHITE/Meadows, farms

LARK SPARROW
Chondestes grammacus
6 inches (15 cm.)

WINGS are brown.
HEAD has chestnut markings set off
by white.
NECK is brown.
BREAST is white with a center spot.
BACK is brown streaked; tail blackish
with white corners.
SEXES are alike.
FEEDS by gleaning.
EATS seeds and insects.
NESTS on the ground.
FLOCKS except when paired for
nesting.
WINTERS in the Gulf Coast and
Mexico.
MIGRATES into Montana by early
May.
MALE OFTEN SINGS AT NIGHT.

KILLDEER
Charadrius vociferus
8 inches (20 cm.)

WINGS are brown.
HEAD has white eye-stripe over dark cheeks.
NECK is white.
BREAST is white with two black bands.
LEGS are long and yellow.
BACK is brown with rust on the rump.
SEXES are alike.
FEEDS by gleaning.
EATS insects.
NESTS on the ground.
WINTERS mostly in southern U.S.
MIGRATES into Montana by late March.
ADULTS PERFORM FALSE-INJURY DISPLAY IF THE NEST IS AP-PROACHED.

53

BROWN

BROWN & WHITE/Moist woodlands, thickets

SWAINSON'S THRUSH
Catharus ustulatus
6-1/4 inches (16 cm.)

WINGS are brown.
HEAD is brown.
NECK is brown.
BREAST is white with brown spots.
BACK is brown.
EYES have a buff eye ring.
SEXES are alike.
FEEDS by swooping and gleaning.
EATS insects and some fruit.
NESTS in a shrub, usually near water.
WINTERS in South America.
MIGRATES into Montana by early May.
DISTINGUISHED FROM SIMILAR THRUSHES BY THE BUFFY EYE RING AND CHEEKS.

RED-TAILED HAWK

Buteo jamaicensis
18 inches (46 cm.)

WINGS are brown.
HEAD is brown.
BILL is hooked.
NECK is brown with a white chin.
BREAST is tan; streaked bellyband is usual.
BACK is brown; tail rust—does not always show from below.
SEXES are alike.
FEEDS by swooping.
EATS rodents, rabbits, and snakes.
NESTS in a tree or on a cliff.
WINTERS in the region.
MIGRATES within the region.
THERE ARE MANY VARIETIES OF PLUMAGE WITHIN THE SPECIES.

55

BROWN & WHITE/Open country

SWAINSON'S HAWK
Buteo swainsoni
18 inches (46 cm.)

WINGS are brown, uptilted in soaring.
HEAD is brown with a white chin.
NECK is brown.
BREAST varies from rust-brown bib to all brown.
BACK is brown.
SEXES are alike.
FEEDS by spotting prey from on high.
EATS rodents and insects.
NESTS in trees or on cliffs.
FLOCKS during migration.
WINTERS in South America.
MIGRATES into Montana by mid-March.
BREAST AND UNDERWINGS VARY FROM BROWN IN DARK PHASE TO WHITE IN LIGHT PHASE.

NORTHERN SHOVELER
Anas clypeata
14 inches (36 cm.)

WINGS have a blue patch.
HEAD is green.
BILL is large and flat, broader at tip.
NECK is green.
BREAST white, noticeable brown sides.
LEGS are orange.
BACK is white with a black stripe.
EYES are yellow.
FEMALE is brown.
FEEDS by straining mud through bill.
EATS aquatic insects, plankton, snails.
NESTS on the ground.
WINTERS southern U.S. to C. Amer.
MIGRATES into Montana by late Mar.
FOUND WORLD-WIDE. OFTEN STIR UP BOTTOM BY CIRCLING IN WATER.

57

BROWN

BROWN & WHITE/Thickets

SONG SPARROW
Melospiza melodia
6 inches (15 cm.)

WINGS are brown.
HEAD is brown with a dark eye-stripe, grayish eyebrow.
NECK is brown-streaked.
BREAST is streaked with large center spot.
BACK is brown-streaked.
SEXES are alike.
FEEDS by gleaning.
EATS insects and seeds.
NESTS on the ground or in a bush.
WINTERS in the Rockies.
PUMPS ITS TAIL IN FLIGHT.

OSPREY
Pandion haliaetus
22 inches (56 cm.)

WINGS are dark brown.
HEAD white with brown eye-stripe,
continuing across cheek.
BILL is hooked.
NECK is brown with a white throat.
BREAST is white.
BACK is dark brown.
EYES are yellow.
FEMALE has a dark necklace.
FEEDS by plunging feet first.
EATS fish.
NESTS in a dead tree, pinnacle or on
the ground near water.
WINTERS from the southern U.S.
southward.
MIGRATES Montana by early April.
SPECIES ALMOST DESTROYED IN
THE 1950'S-1970'S BY DDT.

59

BROWN

BROWN & WHITE/Wetlands

SPOTTED SANDPIPER
Actitis macularia
6 inches (15 cm.)

WINGS are brown.
HEAD is brown with white cheeks.
BILL is long.
NECK is white with dark spots.
BREAST is white with dark spots.
LEGS are light-colored.
BACK is brown.
SEXES are alike.
FEEDS by picking food from mud,
rocks, etc.
EATS insects, worms.
NESTS in the grass.
FLOCKS occasionally in migration.
WINTERS southern U.S. southward.
MIGRATES into Montana in April.
TEETERS CONSTANTLY. SPOTS
DISAPPEAR IN FALL AND WINTER.

WILSON'S PHALAROPE
Phalaropus tricolor
7-1/2 inches (19 cm.)

WINGS are gray with a white stripe.
HEAD is white with blackish eyestripe.
BILL is needle-like and long.
NECK long with a black-gray stripe
shading to cinnamon.
BREAST is cinnamon; belly is white.
LEGS are long and gray.
BACK is gray.
FEMALE is brighter; cinnamon with
eye and neck stripes.
FEEDS both on land and in water.
EATS insects.
NESTS on shore.
WINTERS in South America.
MIGRATES Montana by mid-April.
SEX ROLES REVERSED; FEMALE
COURTS; MALE INCUBATES. THEY
WILL SPIN IN WATER.

61

BROWN

BROWN & WHITE/Woodlands

CHIPPING SPARROW
Spizella passerina
5 inches (13 cm.)

WINGS are brown with two white stripes.
HEAD has a rust cap and a black eye-stripe.
NECK is gray.
BREAST is gray.
BACK is brown-streaked.
SEXES are alike.
FEEDS by gleaning.
EATS insects and seeds.
NESTS in trees.
FLOCKS in the winter.
WINTERS from extreme southern U.S. south into Mexico.
MIGRATES into Mont. by mid-April.
WHEN THE FEMALE STARTS INCUBATING, THE MALE LOOKS FOR A NEW MATE.

WESTERN MEADOWLARK
Sturnella neglecta
8-1/2 inches (22 cm.)

WINGS are brown.
HEAD is brown-and-white striped.
NECK brown, throat yellow.
BREAST is yellow with a black bib.
BACK is brown-streaked.
SEXES are alike.
FEEDS by gleaning.
EATS insects and seeds.
NESTS on the ground
WINTERS from Colorado on south.
MIGRATES into Montana by late February.
SEVEN STATES HAVE NAMED THE MEADOWLARK THEIR STATE BIRD.

63

BROWN

BROWN & YELLOW/Woodlands

WESTERN FLYCATCHER
Empidonax difficilis
5 inches (13 cm.)

WINGS are brown with white bars.
HEAD is olive-brown.
NECK is olive-brown.
BREAST is yellow.
BACK is olive-brown.
EYES have a white ring.
SEXES are alike.
FEEDS by hovering and gleaning.
EATS insects.
WINTERS in Mexico.
MIGRATES into Montana by late May.
NESTS IN MANY PLACES: STREAM
BANKS, TREE CAVITIES, CLIFF
LEDGES, PORCH ROOFS, ETC.

CLARK'S NUTCRACKER
Nucifraga columbiana
11 inches (28 cm.)

WINGS are black with a white patch.
HEAD is gray.
BILL is long.
NECK is gray.
BREAST is light gray.
BACK is gray; black tail has white sides.
SEXES are alike.
FEEDS by gleaning.
EATS pine seeds.
NESTS in trees.
WINTERS in the region.
MIGRATES to lower elevations in the winter.
WILL CACHE 20,000 TO 30,000 SEEDS FOR WINTER FOOD.
SHARES CAMP ROBBER TITLE WITH GRAY JAY.

65

GRAY

GRAY/Evergreens

DARK-EYED JUNCO
Junco hyemalis
5-1/4 inches (13 cm.)

WINGS are brown or gray.
HEAD has a dark gray or black hood.
BILL is yellow.
NECK same as hood.
BREAST is white below throat.
BACK is gray-brown.
SEXES are alike.
FEEDS by gleaning on the ground.
EATS insects and seeds.
NESTS on the ground.
FLOCKS in the winter.
WINTERS in the Rockies.
MIGRATES within the region.
THE FIVE VARIETIES OF JUNCO IN
THIS REGION ARE NOW ALL
KNOWN AS THE DARK-EYED JUNCO.
OREGON PICTURED.

GRAY JAY
Perisoreus canadensis
10 inches (25 cm.)

WINGS are gray.
HEAD has white cheeks and forehead,
black nape.
NECK is light gray.
BREAST is light gray.
BACK and tail are gray.
SEXES are alike.
FEEDS by gleaning.
EATS insects, fruits, and carrion.
NESTS in trees.
WINTERS in the region.
WILL ENJOY YOUR PICNIC—
SHARES TITLE OF CAMP ROBBER
WITH CLARK'S NUTCRACKER.
FORMERLY CALLED CANADA JAY.

67

GRAY

GRAY/Evergreens

MOUNTAIN CHICKADEE
Parus gambeli
4-1/4 inches (11 cm.)

WINGS are gray.
HEAD is black with a white line over the eye.
NECK is white with a black throat.
BREAST is light gray with a tinge of buff at sides.
BACK is gray.
SEXES are alike.
FEEDS by gleaning.
EATS insects and seeds.
NESTS in a tree cavity.
FLOCKS in the winter.
WINTERS in the region.
MIGRATES upward after the breeding season.
WILL FLOCK WITH OTHER SPECIES.

PYGMY NUTHATCH
Sitta pygmaea
3-1/2 inches (9 cm.)

WINGS are gray.
HEAD has a gray-brown cap.
NECK has a white nape spot.
BREAST is cream; throat is white.
BACK is gray.
EYES have a black eye-stripe.
SEXES are alike.
FEEDS by gleaning.
EATS insects and seeds.
NESTS in a tree cavity.
FLOCKS with other species.
WINTERS in the region.
UNMATED MALES HELP BUILD THE
NEST AND CARE FOR THE YOUNG
BIRDS.

69

GRAY

GRAY/Evergreens

RUBY-CROWNED KINGLET

70

Regulus calendula
4 inches (10 cm.)

WINGS have two white bars.
HEAD has a red crown, not always seen.
NECK is gray, white throat.
BREAST light gray, belly light buff.
BACK is gray.
EYES have a white ring.
FEMALE has no red crown.
FEEDS by hovering and gleaning.
EATS insects, sap, berries.
NESTS in trees.
FLOCKS in the winter.
WINTERS in Central America.
MIGRATES into Montana by early May.
BUILDS A HANGING NEST DEEP ENOUGH TO CONCEAL THE INCUBATING PARENT.

WESTERN WOOD-PEWEE
Contopus sordidulus
6 inches (15 cm.)

WINGS are gray-brown.
HEAD is gray-brown.
NECK is gray-brown.
BREAST is olive-gray.
BACK is gray-brown.
SEXES are alike.
FEEDS by fly-catching in air and
gleaning.
EATS insects.
NESTS in trees.
WINTERS in South America.
MIGRATES into Montana by mid-May.
RESEMBLES ITS COUSIN, THE
EASTERN WOOD- PEWEE.

71

GRAY

GRAY/Marshes

GADWALL
Anas strepera
13-1/2 inches (37 cm.)

WINGS are gray with red spot on fore wing.
HEAD is gray.
NECK is gray.
BREAST is gray.
BACK has black rump.
FEMALE has orange bill; lacks black rump.
FEEDS by dabbling.
EATS aquatic plants and creatures.
NESTS on the ground.
WINTERS in southern U.S. and further south.
MIGRATES into Montana by mid-April.
DIVES MORE OFTEN THAN OTHER DABBLERS.

AMERICAN DIPPER
Cinclus mexicanus
5-3/4 inches (15 cm.)

WINGS are gray.
HEAD is gray.
NECK is gray.
BREAST is gray.
BACK is gray.
EYES can look white when bird blinks.
SEXES are alike.
FEEDS underwater.
EATS aquatic insects and small fish.
NESTS in moss or ferns, often under
bridges, rocks at times.
WINTERS in the Rockies.
SWIMS AND FEEDS UNDERWATER.

73

GRAY

GRAY/Wetlands

AMERICAN COOT
Fulica americana
12 inches (30 cm.)

WINGS are darker than the back.
HEAD is black.
BILL is white.
NECK is black.
BREAST is gray.
BACK is gray with a white patch under the tail.
EYES are red.
SEXES are alike.
FEEDS in the water and gleans on shore.
EATS aquatic plants, fish and insects.
NESTS over water in tall vegetation.
WINTERS from Colorado south.
MIGRATES into Montana by late March.
COOTS ARE MEMBERS OF THE RAIL FAMILY.

CANADA GOOSE
Branta canadensis
16 to 25 inches (41 to 64 cm.)

WINGS are gray-brown.
HEAD is black with a white cheek patch.
BILL is black.
NECK is black.
BREAST is pale gray-brown.
BACK is gray-brown.
SEXES are alike.
FEEDS by dipping and grazing.
EATS shoots, roots, grass, and seeds.
NESTS on the ground near water.
FLOCKS are often found in urban parks.
WINTERS throughout the region.
THERE ARE AT LEAST TEN SUB-SPECIES OF THE CANADA GOOSE.

75

GRAY

GRAY/Wetlands

NORTHERN PINTAIL

Anas acuta

18-1/2 inches (47 cm.)

WINGS are brown.
HEAD chocolate; brown cheeks; white stripe in neck.
BILL is dark gray.
NECK is long, white; throat is brown.
BREAST white; sides gray-brown.
BACK is gray-brown with a long, sharp, black tail.
FEMALE brown; belly white.
FEEDS by dipping, gleaning.
EATS seeds, aquatic plants.
NESTS on the ground.
FLOCKS in large numbers.
WINTERS in Colorado south.
MIGRATES into Montana by late Mar.
MOST WIDELY DISTRIBUTED
NORTH AMERICAN DUCK.

GREATER SANDHILL CRANE
Grus canadensis
37 inches (94 cm.)

WINGS are gray.
HEAD has a red cap.
BILL is long and slender.
NECK is long, gray or stained brown.
BREAST is gray or stained brown.
LEGS are very long.
BACK gray or stained brown; tail
tufted. EYES are yellow.
SEXES are alike.
FEEDS by probing, gleaning, in
winter on mown fields.
EATS roots, seeds, small animals, etc.
NESTS on the ground.
FLOCKS except while breeding.
WINTERS southern U.S. and Mexico.
MIGRATE Montana by mid-April.
SANDHILL CRANES HAVE A LONG-
TERM PAIR BOND.

77

GRAY

GRAY/Woodlands or forests, mostly

GREAT HORNED OWL
Bubo virginianus
20 inches (51 cm.)

WINGS are gray.
HEAD is gray with ear tufts.
BILL is hooked.
NECK is short and gray with a white throat.
BREAST is gray, striped with horizontal bars.
LEGS are feathered to the toes.
BACK is gray.
EYES are large and yellow.
SEXES are alike.
FEEDS by swooping down on prey.
EATS rabbits, rodents.
NESTS in a tree.
WINTERS in the region.
BREEDS AND NESTS DURING JANUARY AND FEBRUARY.

AMERICAN ROBIN
Turdus migratorius
8-1/2 inches (22 cm.)

WINGS are gray-brown.
HEAD is dark gray.
NECK is gray with a white throat patch.
BREAST is red.
BACK is gray-brown; tail is the same.
EYES have a white ring.
FEMALE plumage is duller.
FEEDS by gleaning.
EATS worms, insects, and fruit.
NESTS in trees.
WINTERS in Colorado and on south.
MIGRATES into Montana as early as February.
ROBINS LOCATE EARTHWORMS BY SIGHT, NOT SOUND.

79

GRAY

GRAY & RED/Wetlands

REDHEAD
Aythya americana
14-1/2 inches (37 cm.)

WINGS are light gray.
HEAD is red.
BILL is gray with a white ring above a dark tip.
NECK is red.
BREAST is blackish-gray; belly light.
BACK is light gray.
FEMALE is brown.
FEEDS by diving and dabbling.
EATS aquatic vegetation and insects.
NESTS in vegetation over shallow water.
WINTERS in tidewater.
MIGRATES into Montana by late March.
THE FEMALE WILL LAY HER EGGS IN THE NESTS OF OTHER RED-HEADS.

CALIFORNIA GULL
Larus californicus
17 inches (43 cm.)

WINGS gray white borders, black tips.
HEAD is white.
BILL (lower) has a red spot.
NECK is white.
BREAST is white.
LEGS are greenish.
BACK is gray with a white tail.
EYES are dark.
FEEDS by low dives.
EATS worms, mice, garbage, and insects.
NESTS in a scraped cup in the ground.
WINTERS along the Pacific coast.
MIGRATES Montana by late March.
THIS SPECIES MADE FAMOUS WHEN IT HELPED SAVE MORMON CROPS IN UTAH BY FEEDING ON LOCUSTS.

81

GRAY

GRAY & WHITE/Wetlands

RING-BILLED GULL
Larus delawarensis
16 inches (41 cm.)

WINGS are gray with black tips.
HEAD is white.
BILL is yellow with a black ring at tip.
NECK is white.
BREAST is white.
BACK is gray with a white tail.
EYES are yellow with a red ring.
SEXES are alike.
FEEDS by ground gleaning or diving
into water.
EATS fish, worms, insects, bird eggs
and garbage.
NESTS on the ground.
FLOCKS and forms large colonies.
WINTERS as far north as Colorado.
MIGRATES Montana by late April.
WILL OFTEN MATE WITH NEIGH-
BOR FROM THE PREVIOUS YEAR.

WARBLING VIREO
Vireo gilvus
5 inches (13 cm.)

WINGS are brown.
HEAD is gray.
NECK is gray.
BREAST is whitish.
BACK is gray.
EYES have broad white eyestripe.
SEXES are alike.
FEEDS by gleaning.
EATS insects and berries.
WINTERS in Central America.
MIGRATES into Montana by mid-May.
THE MOST COMMON AND WIDE-
SPREAD VIREO IN THE REGION.

GRAY

GRAY & WHITE/Woodlands

WHITE-BREASTED NUTHATCH
Sitta carolinensis
5 inches (13 cm.)

WINGS are gray.
HEAD is black with a white face.
NECK is black with a white throat.
BREAST is white.
BACK is gray, chestnut under the gray tail.
FEMALE plumage is duller.
FEEDS by gleaning tree bark.
EATS insects, acorns, nuts.
NESTS in a tree cavity.
FLOCKS sometimes with chickadees.
WINTERS in the region.
THE PAIR BOND IS STRONG,
PERHAPS FOR LIFE.

MacGILLVRAY'S WARBLER
Oporornis tolmiei
4-1/2 inches (11 cm.)

WINGS are brown
HEAD is gray.
NECK is gray.
BREAST is yellow.
BACK is olive-brown.
EYES have a broken ring.
FEMALE has a lighter-gray head.
FEEDS by gleaning.
NESTS close to ground in vegetation.
WINTERS in Central America.
MIGRATES into Montana by mid-May.
THIS WARBLER HOPS, WHILE ITS
LOOK-ALIKE (CONNECTICUT
WARBLER) WALKS.

85

GRAY

GRAY & YELLOW/Evergreens

YELLOW-RUMPED (AUDUBON'S) WARBLER
Dendroica coronata
5 inches (13 cm.)

WINGS are gray with white patch.
HEAD is black with a yellow crown.
NECK is gray with a yellow throat.
BREAST is black with a white belly.
BACK is gray with a yellow rump.
EYES have a white eye ring.
FEMALE colors are duller.
FEEDS by fly-catching in air and gleaning.
EATS insects and berries.
NESTS in trees.
FLOCKS often.
WINTERS in the southern U.S. and Mexico.
MIGRATES into Montana by late April.
EASTERN YELLOW-RUMPED (MYRTLE) HAS A WHITE THROAT.

TRUMPETER SWAN
Cygnus buccinator
45 inches (114 cm.)

WINGS are white.
HEAD is white.
BILL is black.
NECK is white.
BREAST is white.
BACK is white.
SEXES are alike.
FEEDS by dabbling.
EATS aquatic vegetation and insects.
NESTS usually on a beaver or muskrat house.
SUMMERS and winters in the Yellowstone-Teton area.
IN THIS REGION FOUND ONLY IN THE YELLOWSTONE-TETON AREA.

87

WHITE

WHITE PELICAN
Pelecanus erythrorhynchos
50 inches (127 cm.)

WINGS are white with black tips,
particularly below.
HEAD is white.
BILL is huge and yellow-orange.
NECK is long and white.
BREAST is white.
BACK is white.
SEXES are alike.
FEEDS by scooping with bill.
EATS fish.
NESTS on the ground.
FLOCKS sometimes with cormorants.
WINTERS on the Gulf Coast.
MIGRATES Montana by mid-April.
SECOND CHICK IN BROOD USUALLY
DIES BECAUSE OF HARASSMENT BY
ITS OLDER SIBLING.

YELLOW WARBLER

Dendroica petechia
4 inches (10 cm.)

WINGS are yellow-green with yellow bars.
HEAD is yellow.
NECK is yellow.
BREAST is yellow with red streaks.
BACK is yellow-green.
FEMALE has fewer streaks on the breast.
FEEDS by gleaning on bark and on the ground.
EATS insects.
NESTS in trees.
WINTERS in Mexico and on south.
MIGRATES into Montana by mid-May.
COWBIRDS FREQUENTLY LAY THEIR EGGS IN YELLOW WARBLER NESTS.

89

YELLOW & BLACK/Evergreens

WESTERN TANAGER
Piranga ludoviciana
6 inches (16 cm.)

WINGS are black with yellow or whitish stripes.
HEAD is red.
NECK is yellow below the red.
BREAST is yellow.
BACK is black, with yellow rump and black tail.
FEMALE has green head and back.
FEEDS by gleaning.
EATS insects and fruit.
NESTS in trees.
WINTERS from northern Mexico to Costa Rica.
MIGRATES into Montana by mid May.
ONE OF THE MOST BEAUTIFUL ROCKY MOUNTAIN BIRDS.

AMERICAN GOLDFINCH
Carduelis tristis
4-1/4 inches (11 cm.)

WINGS are black with white patches.
HEAD is yellow with a black forehead.
NECK is yellow.
BREAST is yellow.
BACK is yellow with a black, notched tail, white rump.
FEMALE has olive-brown head and back.
FEEDS in foliage and on the ground.
EATS seeds.
NESTS in trees.
WINTERS in Colorado and the southern Rockies.
MIGRATES into Montana in May.
MALE FEEDS THE FEMALE ON THE NEST. SHE SITS ON THE NEST 95% OF THE TIME.

91

YELLOW

YELLOW & BLACK/Willow shrublands (high elevations)

WILSON'S WARBLER
Wilsonia pusilla
4-1/4 inches (11 cm.)

WINGS are olive.
HEAD is yellow with a black cap.
NECK is olive.
BREAST and throat are yellow.
BACK is olive, with dark tail.
FEMALE lacks the black cap.
FEEDS by hovering and pouncing, and gleaning.
EATS insects.
NESTS near the ground.
WINTERS in Mexico.
MIGRATES into Montana by mid-May.
SUMMERS COAST-TO-COAST IN CANADA, ONLY A MIGRANT EAST OF THE ROCKIES IN THE U.S.

RUFOUS HUMMINGBIRD
Selasphorus rufus
3-1/2 inches (9 cm.)

WINGS are reddish-brown.
HEAD is reddish-brown, green crown.
BILL is long, black.
NECK is copper with orange throat.
BREAST is copper.
BACK is copper.
FEMALE has a green back, copper
sides and throat spots.
FEEDS by hovering.
EATS nectar and insects.
NESTS in trees.
WINTERS in Mexico.
MIGRATES into Montana by late May.
THE ONLY NORTH AMERICAN
HUMMINGBIRD WITH A REDDISH
BACK.

93

MISCELLANEOUS

GREEN/Evergreens

BROAD-TAILED HUMMINGBIRD
Selasphorus platycercus
4 inches (10 cm.)

WINGS are greenish-brown.
HEAD has a metallic-green crown.
BILL is long and black.
NECK is green.
BREAST is white with a red throat patch.
BACK is green.
FEMALE has speckled throat, rusty sides.
FEEDS by hovering.
EATS nectar and spiders.
NESTS in trees.
WINTERS in Mexico.
MIGRATES into Yellowstone by late May.
THIS BIRD IS FOND OF BATHING.

CASSIN'S FINCH
Carpodacus cassinii
6 inches (15 cm.)

WINGS are brown.
HEAD is dark red on top; red ends abruptly at neck.
NECK is brown.
BREAST is reddish.
BACK is streaked olive-gray; tail is notched.
FEMALE is olive-brown with no red, has dark ear patch.
FEEDS in foliage and on the ground.
EATS buds, berries, and seeds.
NESTS in a tree.
FLOCKS throughout the year.
WINTERS from Montana on south.
MIGRATES into Montana in May.
CAN BE DISTINGUISHED FROM HOUSE FINCH BY THE SLIGHTLY DARKER RED CAP ON THE HEAD.

95

MISCELLANEOUS

RED & BROWN/Evergreens

RED CROSSBILL
Loxia curvirostra
5-1/2 inches (14 cm.)

WINGS are brown.
HEAD is red.
BILL has crossed mandibles.
NECK and BREAST are red.
BACK is red.
FEMALE brown with white throat,
yellow breast and rump.
FEEDS by gleaning.
EATS seeds from cones, buds.
NESTS in trees.
WINTERS in the region.
MIGRATES to lower elevations for the
winter.
MAY BE RIGHT- OR LEFT-
"HANDED", DEPENDING UPON HOW
THE BILL CROSSES. USES BILL TO
PRY OPEN SCALES OF CONES.

HOUSE FINCH
Carpodacus mexicanus
5-1/4 inches (13 cm.)

WINGS are brown.
HEAD is red.
NECK is brown; throat is red.
BREAST is red above brown-streaked belly.
BACK is brown.
FEMALE is brown with streaked throat and breast.
FEEDS by gleaning.
EATS seeds and fruit.
NESTS in shrubs.
FLOCKS after breeding.
WINTERS in the region.
UNCOMMON IN THE NORTHERN ROCKIES.

97

MISCELLANEOUS

RUST/Wetlands

RUDDY DUCK
Oxyura jamaicensis
11 inches (28 cm.)

WINGS are red.
HEAD has a black cap, white cheeks.
BILL bright blue summer, darker winter.
NECK is rust.
BREAST is rust.
BACK is rust.
FEMALE is brown, with dark line across whitish cheek.
FEEDS by diving.
EATS aquatic vegetation, insects.
NESTS above water in marshy vegetation.
WINTERS in Central America.
MIGRATES into Montana by early April.
AIR SACK IN MALE'S NECK INFLATED WHEN COURTING.

FERRUGINOUS HAWK

Buteo regalis
23 inches (59 cm.)

WINGS brown with white underneath.
HEAD is brown-streaked.
BILL has a sharp hook.
NECK is brown-streaked.
BREAST is white with rust spots.
LEGS are rust-feathered to the toes.
BACK is rust; tail is whitish.
EYES are yellow.
SEXES look alike.
FEMALE is larger.
FEEDS by swooping on prey.
EATS rabbits and rodents.
NESTS in a tree or rock outcropping.
SUMMERS in Colorado north to
southern Canada.
WINTERS from Colorado south.
LIKE BLACK SHEEP, ABOUT 10%
ARE "MORPHS."

99

MISCELLANEOUS

INDEX OF COMMON NAMES

Avocet, American 12

Blackbird, Brewer's 3
    Red-winged 5
    Yellow-headed 19

Bluebird, Mountain 21
    Western 24

Bunting, Lazuli 25

Chickadee, Black-capped 17
    Mountain 68

Coot, American 74

Cowbird, Brown-headed 6

Crane, Greater Sandhill 77

Crow, American 7

Crossbill, Red 96

Dipper, American 73

Dove, Mourning 44

Duck, Ruddy 98

Eagle, Bald 50
    Golden 33

Falcon, Prairie 49

Finch, Cassin's 95
    House 97
    Rosy 37

Flicker, Northern 45

Flycatcher, Western 64

Gadwall 72

Goldfinch, American 91

Goose, Canada 75

Grebe, Pied-billed 43
    Western 14

Grosbeak, Black-headed 8
    Evening 18

Gull, California 81
    Ring-billed 82

Hawk, Ferruginous 99
    Red-tailed 55
    Swainson's 56

Heron, Great Blue 27

Hummingbird, Broad-tailed 94
    Rufous 93

Jay, Gray 67
    Scrub 22
    Steller's 20

Junco, Dark-eyed 66

Kestrel, American 29

Killdeer 53

Kingfisher, Belted 31

Kinglet, Ruby-crowned 70

Magpie, Black-billed 15

Mallard 42

Meadowlark, Western 63

Merganser, Common 10

Nighthawk, Common 36
Nutcracker, Clark's 65
Nuthatch, Pygmy 69
    Red-breasted 30
    White-breasted 84
Osprey 59
Owl, Great Horned 78
Pelican, White 88
Phalarope, Wilson's 61
Pintail, Northern 76
Ptarmigan, White-tailed 39
Raven, Common 4
Redhead 80
Robin, American 79
Sandpiper, Spotted 60
Sapsucker, Red-naped 16
    Williamson's 2
Shoveler, Northern 57
Siskin, Pine 51
Sparrow, Chipping 62
    House 32
    Lark 52
    Lincoln's 48
    Song 58
    White-crowned 47
Starling, European 1

Swallow, Barn 23
    Tree 28
    Violet-green 26
Swan, Trumpeter 87
Tanager, Western 90
Teal, Blue-winged 41
Thrush, Hermit 35
    Swainson's 54
Towhee, Green-tailed 38
    Rufous-sided 11
Vireo, Warbling 83
Warbler, MacGillvray's 85
    Wilson's 92
    Yellow 89
    Yellow-rumped (Audubon's) 86
Wigeon, American 40
Wren, House 46
    Rock 34
Wood-Pewee, Western 71
Woodpecker, Downy (or Hairy) 9

NOTES: